I THE BLACK POET COMES

JAMES M. MOTEN

Printed in the United States of America

ISBN 979-8-89114-184-1 (hc)
ISBN 979-8-89114-183-4 (sc)
ISBN 979-8-89114-185-8 (e)

Library of Congress Pre-assigned Control Number: 2025905734

2025.04.24

MainSpring Books
5901 W. Century Blvd
Suite 750
Los Angeles, CA, US, 90045

www.mainspringbooks.com

I THE BLACK POET COMES

About the author: *James Marvin Moten was born November 12th, 1947, in Crockett, Texas about nine miles from the Louisiana border. He is the tenth child of fourteen born of the union of Spencer Moten Sr, and Arlishie Harris Moten. Around the age of five his mother took him, his older brother Peter and baby sister Delma with her, and hitch hiked a ride with a friendly Caucasian couple from New York who took the impoverished family all the way to Tucson, Arizona.*

Arlishie Harris Moten steadfastly refused to let her younger children grow up in highly racial sensitive Crockett, Texas. She was proven extremely correct, because one son performed autopsies at Tucson Medical Center at sixteen years of age. Future Doctor perhaps? A daughter is now Dr Darlene Moten, another daughter holds a degree and is the author of several bestselling books in addition to having her own television talk show. Another son is the youngest member to enter the multi-million dollar insurance board of a top insurance firm.

James, is a retired IRS Agent, has three honorable discharges, served in both the United States Air Force, and United States Marine Corps (Iceland). He owns a finance degree, is the author of I IRS (MY HELL OF LIFE). James Owns his own tax corporation.

James wrote the poems several decades ago in relationship to his life's experiences at the time. He wrote the poem's using popular street language of the time. One poem, 'Twenty-four hours of love (Then a little over time) was put to country western music, which was not pursued due to the company's problems at the attorney general level of New York. Another poem, 'Slave' is cherished by everyone including scholars whom he let read it as a crowning achievement. Another poem written at the height of the Vietnam War is soldiers prayer', which was written in Iceland.

James downloaded images from pictures posted by google when he organized, ' I THE BLACK POET COMES" in 2023. He downloaded the free images with the utmost respect in an effort to portray the deep meaning of the poems written decades ago.

James is an adamant believer in the existence of God and owes any success he has achieved in his hell of life to his precious mother and God.

James dedicates this book of poems to Arlishie Harris Moten, the greatest person to walk the face of the earth.

CONTENTS

THE PLANET SOUL

Somewhere out there in the dark of night
Lies a planet truly out of sight
Let your imagination go and take you there
From here or anywhere

As you begin to get near
Soulful sounds pierce your ears
As you get closer your heart pounds
To the beat of rhythmic sounds

There's JAMES BROWN off to your right
Soul Brother number one knows he is out of sight
SMOKEY ROBINSON'S is trailing his tracks of tears
You know of his great songs throughout the years

JAMES M. MOTEN
1

Tina Turner, TIna Turner, Tina Turner, Tina Turner
In your heart, I see the star of every night and every day
In your eyes, I get lost, I get washed away
Just as long as I'm here in your arms
I could be in no better place

Tina thank you for the above words
Soul sister supreme
You are simply the best
Proudly walk on streets made of gold

Mrs. ARETHA FRANKLIN soul sister supreme
As I take a closer look I see what you mean.
Spanish Harlem sounds dancing through the streets
This is one soul sister you can't beat

As you look around everyone is doing their thing
Do you see what I see FREDA PAYNE holding a solid gold string
Singing bring the boys home
I'd like to go home, man would I like to go home

MARTHA REEVES and the VANDELLAS
Hello fella
MARTHA, since my name is JIMMY
Do you remember that song "JIMMY MACK"
Why don't you hurry back? Yes!
I'm back!

The fabulous BOBBY WOMACK is listening
He said he couldn't hear a dam thing
Cause he's California Dreaming
In such a soulful way

There's JERRY BUTLER sitting on a block of ice
Hey, JERRY, how is everything
A little cold JIMMY, but only the strong survive
This planet's out of sight

123----123—MR WILSON PICKETT
When was the last time you went to the land of 1000 dances
Not lately JIMMY, but I'm going soon, because it will be 1001
I'm adding the breakdown.

YESTERDAY'S LOVE

This is just a few lines to let you know just how I feel.
I never loved many people in my life
But I had plans of making you forever my wife
You were always too busy to even give me a smile
Stand close to me and talk for awhile

Hey girl it's too late for me to be with you
My time has passed, I took my life!
I only wish you could have been forever my wife

JAMES M. MOTEN   3

The world you come from they wouldn't have understood
They wouldn't let a woman be a woman
And a man be a man, So I rest my case from the human race
And lock myself away to the end of time

Hey girl it's too late for me to be with you
My time has passed, I took my life!
I only wish you could have been forever my wife
As I slowly bow my head, it's time for me to go

Come see me please this place gets awful lonely
If you happen to feel something softly touch your lovely face
Don't get frightened my love
Its only me reaching out from my new world, this place

THERE WERE THE TIMES

There were the times
I felt like giving up
I cannot turn salt right into gold
Laying my head up
And wishing I was old

But a man cannot sit around
Sit right down and turn aside
All of his misfortunes
And run away and hide

There were the times
When I could plunder
Right into and open grave
and turn off into a forever peaceful gaze

But a man cannot lay around
Lay right down and turn aside
All of his misfortunes
And run away and hide

There were the times
When a man has to stand tall
No matter how the winds may blow
Stand as straight as a brick wall
Come rain, sleet, or snow

But a man cannot stand around
Stand right up and turn aside
All of his misfortunes
And run away and die.

There were the times when this funky life
Got hot and started to smell
A man would give his right arm
From being cased right into hell

Give it up, stand tall
Don't hang around all day
Thinking about your misfortunes
There will be a brighter day

I'M A LONELY MAN

Get up in the morning
Fix myself something to eat
Get myself together
And hit those same old crowed New York streets

I'm a lonely man
I really do not got nowhere to go
I'm a lonely man
Trying hard to make a show

The unemployment line
Gets longer and longer
My ex-wife and kids
Get hungrier and hungrier

Every time I come around
She asks where's your paycheck
I say baby, you have to
Take a postdated check

I'm a lonely man
I really don't got nowhere to go
I'm a lonely man
Trying to make some kind a show

I've tried dealing in dope
But the New York police wouldn't let me show
Attorney Bragg came down on my case
Either you or that dope has to go

The welfare is funky
Food stamps they said no
I knocked up some young girl
And now the judge said I got to show

I'm a lonely man
I really don't have anywhere to go
I'm a lonely man
To lonely to make a show

I WILL LOVE HER ANYWAY

ID 256942165 © peopleimages

Around my tech school people would say
You see that lovely girl she is gay
Although she is pretty as can be
She has no more interest in me

If that's the life that she choose
I wish her the best of luck anyway
It's a life that she can use
To get her love and earn her pay

Gay girl, gay girl
What you learning to do now
Gay girl, gay girl
You know I love you anyhow

I saw your mother yesterday
She said, tell Jimmy she still loves me anyway
The life with me she couldn't use
She said your heart she couldn't bruise

She said she choose this life to live
Push it up and make it thrive
That she doesn't expect the world to be
A lonely place for me

Gay girl, gay girl
What are you learning to do now
Gay girl, gay girl
You know I love you anyhow

People around and about the town
They just don't understand
How a woman loves another woman
And not another man

Even though my heart is broken
I don't have much to say
The world is a tough, tough place
And gay people will have their day

MOTHER WHERE ART THOU

Two women are standing on a Tucson corner
Suddenly One disappears and the other one is left

Two brothers are sitting at the kitchen table at home
Suddenly One is left alone the other one gone

This is God's time
When nothing is yours nor mine

MOTHER' MOTHER' MOTHER
Where art thou?

MOTHER' MOTHER' MOTHER'
Please don't leave me

It's too late my child
Your mother is gone

Where? To be with God
On his gorgeous heavenly throne

Don't shed a tear
She taught you. That it is God you must fear

When times were sadly dark
She was always there
To hold you close
And whisper beautiful thoughts of encouragements in your ear

Don't you be so aggrieved Jimmy
Don't you even worry
For your Mother's is happy in her gorgeous heavenly home
In a place where beautiful angels roam next to God on his throne

Be happy for her
There will be no more tears, sorrow, she will suffer
She'll get a wonderful new body
So exceptionally beautiful
That all of heaven will light up and gleam
When she walks those beautiful streets of gold
Then all of heaven will fill with beautiful music when she talks so bold

KEEP BODY AND SOUL TOGETHER

Don't let your body and mind go to waste
With quick decisions made in violent haste
You're the center of a beautiful flower

Cause you're the future of soul power

Don't lose your temper, clustered in a black flock
Cause you'll be wasting time in a cell block
Your talents are the greatest American's seen
Take a look at Black progress and see what I mean

I know our ancestors , they had it rough
But we wouldn't be here today if they weren't so tough
Their blood has stained the World's soil
As they worked, and fault through all that racial turmoil

Brothers, Sisters I know you say
That violence listens and is the only way
Take a look around you and see mighty mountains of living proof
That we all can make it under a new roof

We can make it in the American system
Just go to school and get that precious wisdom
Keep body and soul together
Everything will get great forever and ever

I FELL IN LOVE WITH THE WOMAN WHO WORKED THE BLOCK

I just don't know how it happened.
Everything was simply great, and my wrap always worked.
I was a playboy known all over Las Vegas town.
There wasn't a single girl throughout I hadn't chased down.

It happened on a groovy night
She stood on the MGM block and whispered to me, ten and two
She was so fine and truly out of sight
Before I realized it, within her arms I flew

I fell in love with the woman who worked the Las Vegas block
And to this day our love is solid as a rock
I've dedicated my entire life to this woman
Much to my surprise I find I'm a better man

My friends say Jimmy you're a fool
To fall in love and marry such a used tool
But you meet love in the strangest of ways
Ways that have been the beginning of my sunny days

Please don't look down on me brother
Please don't look down on me sister
When love enters your door
Other earthly desires you'll have no more

I fell in love with the woman who worked the Las Vegas block
And to this day our love is solid as a rock
I've dedicated my whole life to this woman
Much to my surprise I found I'm an even better man

THESE FUNKY SHOES

Looking down at my size six feet
I fine, they're not to neat
Holes and my feet showing everywhere
I wish I had another pair

These use to belong to someone else
I wish they had kept them themselves
They don't fit right anyway
Maybe I can throw them away someday

These funky shoes, man do they stank
I don't know who to thank
The salvation Army or my older brother hand me downs you know
Gets passed from Dow to Dow

These funky shoes, without them I guess
My feet would be totally insight
Oh well, I guess my mother's right
Ware "em" shut up don't fight
I guess I will have to didn't you

THE GIRL I WANT

I see the gorgeous girl I want
Lovely and full of exciting love
I see the girl I want
Did she come from heaven above

Standing alone and no one on her mind
No one paying any attention to her
Drinking away and thinking about the time
Is she the girl I want for me

I see the girl I want
Lovely and full of wonderous love
I see the girl I want
God knows she's from heaven above

Now if she would just dance with me
There just might be a chance
For the stars above have aligned our romance
For me and her Forever more
Oh God, please let my wish come true

I see the girl I want
So Lovely and full of exciting love
I see the girl I want
God knows she's from heaven above

It won't be long
I'm almost there
I can almost feel
Her smooth and beautiful afro hair
Wait, some guy is just ahead of me
He has the same thoughts as me you see
And now I've lost that girl for me

I saw the girl I loved
That beautiful girl I loved
Lovely and full of exciting love
I saw the girl I wanted
From heaven above

GO AHEAD AND LEAVE I WON'T CRY

It's been a hard lifetime living with you
Things were so bad sometimes I just didn't know what to do
As you pack your bags to leave
I'm not going to stop you cause your love I no longer need

Go ahead and leave, I won't cry
Go ahead and leave, I won't even try
Even though I'll be without love I'll survive
Cause Love and hate mixed together will never thrive

I can't stand your mother anyway
And your brothers and sisters can go their separate way
I've been hurt and treated so horribly bad
Life with you has been so sad

Go ahead and leave, I won't cry
Go ahead and leave, I won't even try
Even though I'll be without love I'll survive
Cause Love and hate mixed together will never thrive

Fussing and fighting all of the time
All this hell raising has blown my mine
Hurry up and catch your jet plane
If not a jet plane then the very next train

Go ahead and leave I won't cry
Go ahead and leave I won't even try
Even though I'll be without love I'll survive
Cause Love and hate mixed will never thrive

WE CAN'T STOP NOW

We got a taste of restricted honey
And making just a little more money
We can see God's luxurious mountain top
Now I know we can't stop

Four hundred years of toil and trouble
Are mostly behind us now in burned up rubble
We must keep on reaching for that lofty shelf up high
Everyone knows the horrible reasons why

Times are starting to change
We must get ready to re-arrange
Set up character ourselves
Up, up on those lofty lavish Washington D.C. shelves

We must go to the best schools
So no one can claim we are uneducated fools
But when America decides to turn around and take's a second look
And see how great we've become, it's going to be too late to book

THE JUDGE

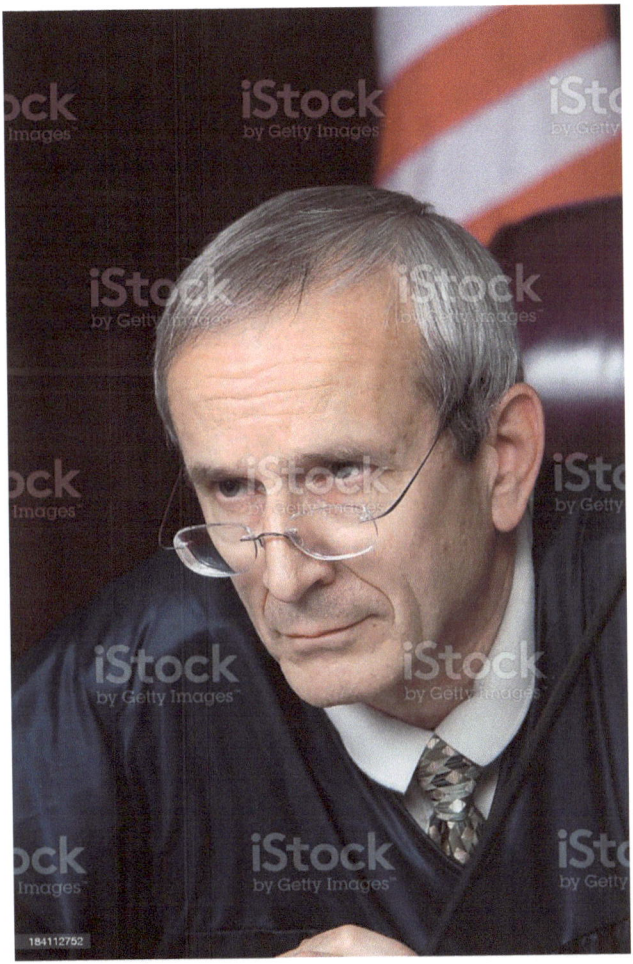

Your honor Judge Thomas, I stand before you
Waiting to see what you're going to do
I've been falsely accused
About something I didn't abuse

Your honor He's a liar, he's the father of my child
He's the only one I've been with all the while
He's got his nerve to stand before you, so tall and slim
When all the time he knows it was him

Well Mr. Moten how do you plead
Was it you who done this fatherly deed
I know one thing you won't be freed
Cause that child's mouth you will feed

Your honor Justice Thomas it wasn't only me
There were several others you see
It was because of her fantastic democratic charms
That this beautiful child's is in her arms

She called to me as I walked by
She said come here little boy
I have something I want you to see
It's a great wonderful, beautiful toy

Unknowingly your honor I entered in her open door
She started to show me much, much more
She said, little boy let me see your toy
She screamed, you are not at all a small boy

She then enclosed me with in her love
It seemed like something from heaven above
When it was all over
I felt several years older

Now I stand here before your bench and you
For something I feel I didn't do
Your free to go young man, go back to school
But never again come under my rule

A LOVELY WHITE DOVE

I was out late one Tampa night
I saw a white dove truly out of sight
I thought she wouldn't be interested in me
Then she said her name was Jeanie

I creeped a little closer and began my military wrap
At first, I thought I would get a slap
But no, she began to unfold
I said, I'll pick you up at eight and I won't be late

That Scorpion she was drinking
I thought had messed up her thinking
It was in a great big jar
With Gin, Vodka, and whatever from afar

The next night I took her on a date
Man I wasn't a minute late
We went out to this Florida place
Far, far from disgrace

With long blonde hair
That hung from here to there
With Saturn blue eyes and shapely hips
One more second I was going to kiss her lips

I began to wonder
If this was the white Dove that Noah sent
I was hoping she would forever be a very close friend
And end up forever in my den

Later on I was wrong
And singing a sad, sad song
I thought I could forever make love
To such a lovely white Dove

GOD PLEASE DAM THE PUSHER MAN

God, please dam the pusher man
He walks around carrying death in his hand
He steals people's lives a little at a time
God knows he will never get mines

Many thought it was their way out
Something to make them forget domination
Something to make them joyfully shout
It's too late America to change combination

Many times over I know drug addicted Americans wish
That they never seen the bitch
Left to swim like a waterless fish
In a fentanyl world with a habit they can't ditch

Here he comes now carrying his bags of death
Every day it will take some American's last breath
For a little while, it makes them forget their tough life
But shortly after, they feel's the same old strife

Each time his price gets higher and higher and higher
Without the consent of the economically hopeless buyer
He knows people will do anything to have it
Steal, gamble, prostitute or even sell rat shit

God please dam the pusher man
He's got to be Satan's right hand
Riding his massive fire breathing death horse of gray
He's already taken millions of people's sunshine away

Oh God please, please hear me
Oh God please hear my deep heart ,plea
Dam the pusher man
Take away the bags of death he carries in his hand

SHE IS MY BACKFIELD WOMAN

Maybe you've seen my woman
Driving about the town
The grape vine has gotten back to me
GI's claim She's the best thing around

She's my backfield woman
And she knows she is driving me wild
There isn't anything I can do
Except sit here crying all the while

Soldier boys, Marines, Airmen while you're gone overseas
Your backfield woman
Will have you on your knees
She'll drive your expensive car all over town
Making sure she's covered all the cities' around

Cause she's my backfield woman
And she knows she's driving me wild
There isn't anything I can do
Except sit here crying all the while

So listen carefully to what I have to say
Don't leave a backfield woman to stay
She proudly signed your Dear John letter
Lied to you on the phone that you are much better

Listen to me soldier Boys, Marines, Airmen as I pray
God help you to never leave a backfield woman
To stay to day or any day

SLAVE

That wretched slave ship made of wood and paste
That I was tossed into in a violent haste
I thought I was in hell for eternity
Then one day I was some-what free

It took hell, blood, and nearly all my guts to survive
I was mostly bones when I arrived
When well I was rushed onto a high platform
There I was sold to the bidder with the quickest arm

I was only in my year twenty-two
The man yelled "nigger" you got fifty years to do
I wasn't sure what he meant
One thing for sure he had not my-consent

The years that follow
They all seemed ghostly hollow
Slavery tore at my throat
Tightly wrapped around me as my black skin coat

I learned that there was a mighty God
To me this seemed quite odd
A God that I could not see
How was he going to free me

I learned of a man called Moses
Who had lead some of God's people free
I begin to wonder
If there was a Moses for me

Then one day great news came my way
Of a great presentation
Someone called a President
Had signed a new proclamation

Since I couldn't read
I could not concede
Then I heard someone shout
That a great bloody civil war had broken out

They said that President Lincoln was determined to see
That I was finally set free
For the next four years
Throughout the South there were a great many tears

When the bloody war was all ended, I was really free
To work on my own and determine my destiny
But deep, deep down in my soul I somehow knew
That the future was going to be very rough for me and you

MY BROTHER JAMES

MY BROTHER BILLIE

MY BROTHER

It was the summer of 1862
I had just turned twenty-two
I told my mother I was going down south to fight
Join the Union Army and die for what's right

She said, James you're free now
You don't have to go down south anymore
I only wish your brother Billie was here
So I won't have to grieve anymore

I joined the Union Army anyway
We marched off the very next day
The training it was swift and fast
Before I knew it the North had past
But the words of my mother would rang in my ear

She would say James, you're free now
You don't have to go down south anymore
I only wish your brother Billie was here
So I won't have to grieve anymore

I never seen my brother Billie
My mother said he'd probably look a lot like me
Just after he was born
He was sold to plantation Hawthorne
As we marched, the words of my mother
would come to me again and again

She would say, James you're free now
You don't have to go down south anymore
I only wish your brother Billie was here
So I won't have to grieve anymore

We fought paste the mason dixie rebel line
The Union Colonel yelled, if we can take bunker hill
This bloody civil war battle's mine
The fighting was intense and hand to hand
A rifle bullet fired at close range went through my chest fired by a tall black rebel man
As I was falling I fired my rifle and he fell dead

We had killed each other
Without ever knowing
We were from the same mother

She would often say, James you're free now
You don't have to go down south anymore
I only wish your brother Billie was here
So I won't have to grieve anymore

DEDICATION TO THE BLACK WOMEN OF THE WORLD

You've Walked on streets made of gold
The hardship of your mountainous stories are already told
You are the Black Diamonds and gold to
God's built heaven and earth around you

For it was you who have toiled for countless hours
Cleaning kitchens and setting flowers
We owe our lives
To someone who has survived so much strife

Your trials and tribulations have risen Mt Everest high
That the figure will stretch beyond the highest sky
You're a lovely bundle of joy and love
You've made it to God's heaven above

For 300 years or more
You worked from rich door to rich door
Mopping kitchens and cleaning vast floors
Till sweat ran freely from your pores

But finally your day has come
You've been molded into the greatest ones
As your radiant beauty shines out right
Soul sister supreme you are truly out of sight

WEDNESDAY'S CHILD

Born into this world of hate
You don't know your destiny nor fate
Fenced in and filled with gloom
There must be a way out of this rat infested room
Tomorrow to the world it is just another day
But for you, it's survival some way
Born in the middle of the meek
Born on the third day of the week
Wednesday's child knows no harmony
The clatter of toys or laughter you see
Wednesday's child is doomed to woe
Wednesday's child has no place to go
Wednesday's child is poor and ragged
Look closely America and see Wednesday's child is you and me

I WOULD HEAR MY MOTHER CRY

When I was a small boy
With very little to eat not even a toy
I would hear my mother say
Jimmy there will be a better day
She used to hide and cry
I was too young to know the multiple reasons why
As the tears would run down her face
She would say Jimmy, one day you'll have to run this race
I would hear my mother cry
I was too young to care, nor did I try
She would sit and figure out how to make it some way
Knowing we would have to eat the next day
As I grew older I finally understood why
I used to hear my mother cry
It's a hard life we have to face
One thing for sure I can win this race

YOU'RE THE STAR OF THE SHOW

Sitting before the glamorous mirror, putting on opaque
Getting yourself ready to go out on the Apollo stage
Brightening up your eyes, polishing your gorgeous lips
Getting ready to put on a super show and make all the people flip

You're the star of the show
And wherever you go, LA or Chicago
Millions of People will be turning out
Singing, dancing, and starting to shout

You Do your marvelous thing out of sight
You break into a beautiful rhythmic tone outright
Thousands of Bright lights shining all about you
You fall back as you do your thing knowing what to do

You're the star of the show
And wherever you go
People will be turning out
Singing, dancing, and starting to shout

As you do your final fling
Everyone is dangling by your solid gold string
As you leave the massive stage and toss a kiss
Not one single person you did miss

You're the star of the show
And wherever you go
People will be turning out
And that's without a doubt

You're the star of the show
And wherever you go
People will be turning out
Singing, dancing, and starting to shout

MONDAY THE WORST DAY OF THE WEEK

shutterstock.com · 78181600

I hate Mondays, most of all
On Mondays, I just can't stand tall
I really rather be,
On some other day of the week

On Monday I have the blues
On Monday, it's all just bad news
I'd rather be
On some other day of the week

Monday is the worst day of the week
It's the day reserved for the meek
I'd rather just stay in bed
And rest my weary head

I hate Mondays most of all
I hate Mondays, take the calendar off the wall
That's a day that should be blank
Left open for me to thank

On Monday I'm just no use
On Monday I just can't show
There's so many other places I rather be
Than on this the first day of the week

Monday is the worst day of the week
It's the day for the meek
I'd rather just stay in bed
And rest my weary head

They should just move that day
Replace it some way
I hate Monday most of all

EVERYBODY'S GOING CRAZY

Take a look around you
Check out the scenes
Brothers and sisters
You'll see what I mean

Everybody's going crazy
They're losing their minds
Everybody's going crazy
They're losing their grip
Everybody's going crazy
America's is starting to slip

People jumping off suicide walls
Leaping from buildings ten stories tall
We're being fed tons of fentanyl dope
Even glazed isotope

Everybody's going crazy
They're losing their minds
Everybody's going crazy
They're losing their grip
Everybody's going crazy
The World is starting to slip

People killing one another
Because of their color
It must be the end of my time
I'm starting to lose my mind

Everybody's going crazy
They're losing their minds
Everybody's going crazy
They're losing their grip
Everybody's going crazy
They're starting to slip

How about you do you feel yourself going
Everything in front of you kaleidoscope glowing
Do you feel yourself being solidified
It won't be long before the world commits suicide

Everybody's gone crazy
They've lost their minds
Everybody's gone crazy
They've lost their grip
Everybody's going crazy
America has already slipped

WHEN I GROW UP I'M GOING TO MARRY YOU

I remember when I was a small boy
Sitting on my front porch playing with my Disneyland toy
I'd see the gorgeous girls as they walked past
I'd yell at them, hey girl's don't walk so fast
I got something to say that will last

I yell out to them when I grow up I'm going to marry you
Cause you look so good and true
Girls' until the sun won't shine anymore
It's going to be me and you forever more

They'd yell back at me, little boy you don't understand
Wait until you're a grown up man
I'd bow my head and slowly walk away
Feeling very sure I'd have my day
The years past fast and before I knew it
I was tall and strong and ready to do it

Then those same girls came walking past
This time they weren't walking so fast
I yelled out to them hey! Do you remember me
They stopped and turned in amazement and yelled that's Jimmy

LIVE FOR TODAY
(HOPE FOR TOMORROW)

It's early in the mourning
And I haven't had nothing to eat
Time for me to start wondering
Down those same old Philadelphia ghetto streets
A Great Life for me has been a mirage
You see it in the distance, but you never meet

So I live for today (hope for tomorrow)
Cause tomorrow might bring nothing but sorrow
My life is filled with aches and pains
And I can feel grief running through my veins

The shadows of the ghetto they seem to haunt me
Giving me a feeling that I will never be free
If God is up there I hope he's looking
At this place that keeps on hooking
Young people like me and you
Keeping us from better things to do

So I live for today (hope for tomorrow)
Cause tomorrow might bring nothing but sorrow
My life is filled with aches and pains
And I can feel grief running through my veins

I look up and the sun is rising
Out beyond the new horizon
I'll wake up one morning and something good will come my way
And God willing I'll leave this burned out Philadelphia Ghetto that day

TWENTY FOUR HOURS OF LOVE
(THEN A LITTLE OVER TIME)

Such a beautiful day
Someone up above knows I'm in love
Today marriage comes my way
Soon I'll be before the throne of love
She holds the only place in my heart
I'll love that girl till death do us part

Twenty four hours of love
She'll be guaranteed
Then a little over time, yes indeed
Then I'll give her all the extra love
She will need

My love is here to stay
Today and everyday
It will grow stronger by the hour
Blossom wide as a new spring flower

Twenty four hours of love
She'll be guaranteed
Then a little over time yes indeed
Then I'll give her all the extra love
She will need

We'll be inseparable
Always together as one
We'll be capable
Of all love when it's said and done

Twenty four hours of love
She'll always be guaranteed
Then a little over time yes indeed
Then I'll give her all the extra love
She will need

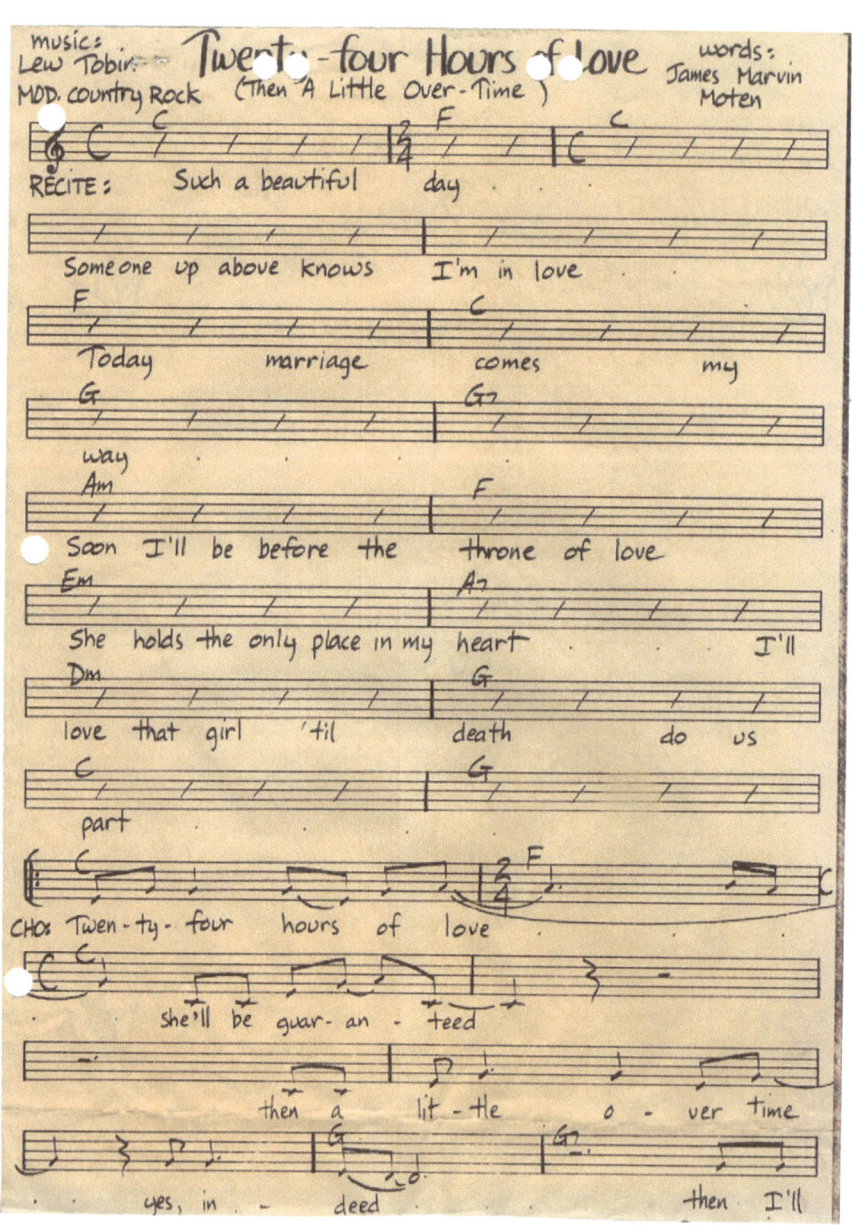

Twenty-four Hours of love (Then A Little Over-Time)

music: Lew Tobin
MOD. Country Rock
words: James Marvin Moten

RECITE: Such a beautiful day

Someone up above knows I'm in love

Today marriage comes my

way

Soon I'll be before the throne of love

She holds the only place in my heart I'll

love that girl 'til death do us

part

CHO: Twen-ty-four hours of love

she'll be guar-an-teed

then a lit-tle o-ver time

yes, in-deed then I'll

I THE BLACK POET COMES

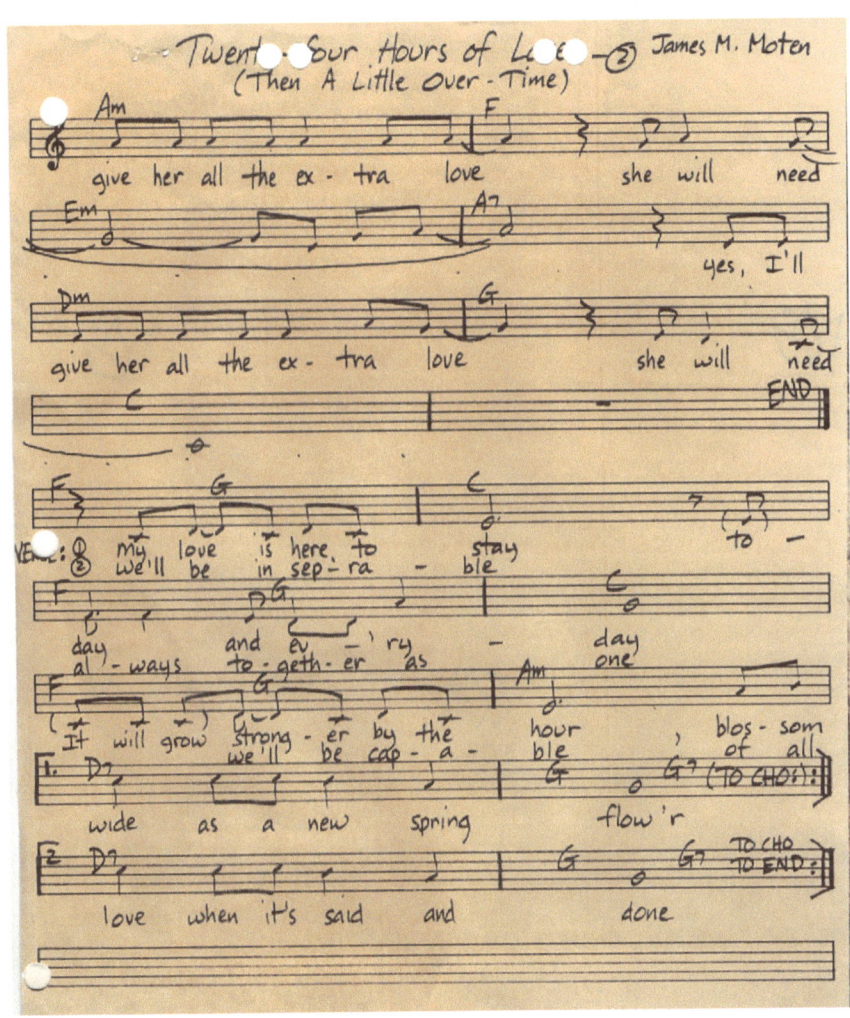

Twenty Four Hours of Love (Then A Little Over-Time) — James M. Moten

give her all the ex-tra love she will need
yes, I'll
give her all the ex-tra love she will need END

my love is here to stay
we'll be in-sep-ra-ble
to
day and ev-'ry day
al-ways to-geth-er as one
It will grow strong-er by the hour, blos-som of all
we'll be cap-a-ble
wide as a new spring flow'r
love when it's said and done

IT'S THE SEASON FOR LOVE

As we walk hand in hand
Through the meadows, beach, and green grassland
I'll pluck a rose
And Place it in your hair through which the beautiful wind blows

The song birds are singing a beautiful soulful melody
They seemed to arrange it just for you and me
As I hold you near as our hearts simultaneously beats
A rhythmic tone so neat

My love is Pacific ocean deep, my love is Atlantic ocean wide
Surely you will remain forever by my side
As The sun shines golden all around us
Making a lovely scene so robust

I lean over and whisper in your ear, I love you
You soulfully hug me ever so tenderly gently
I feel the warmth of your gorgeous lustrous body next to minds
It all most makes me forget about the time

It's that time of the year
When all the worlds love is near
When everything is at our command
It's the season for love

FREEDOM HAS A PRICE

TO SOAR HIGH LIKE THE FLIGHT OF A GOLDEN EAGLE
GRACEFULLY, SILENTLY, AND SWIFTLY ALONG IT'S FLIGHT SO FREE
DOMINATED BY NO ONE, NOR THE MEEK, OR FEEBLE
THE EAGLE IS FREEDOM'S ULTIMATE SYMBOL, CAUSE FREEDOM IS IT'S PLEA

THERE ARE THOSE WHO WOULD LOVE TO ENTER THE EAGLES MIGHTY DOMAIN
TO END ITS UNIVERSAL FLIGHT THAT IS SO FREE
TAKE AWAY IT'S FREEDOM AND MAKE THINGS NOT THE SAME
DESTROY THIS MIGHTY SYMBOL YOU SEE

THE EAGLE KNOWS THAT FREEDOM HAS A PRICE
TO CRUSH AND DEFEAT IT'S MANY FOE
NOT ONCE, BUT TWICE
TO STRIKE UPON THEM A MIGHTY SHATTERING BLOW

EAGLES HAVE DIED DEFENDING THIS LAND
THEIR BLOOD HAS RAN FREELY ON CLIFFS, BEACHES, AND FOREIGN GREEN GRASSLANDS
THEY KNEW THE PRICE AND PAID IT SWIFTLY
THE PRICE OF OUR FREEDOM WAS PAID BY THEIR LIVES

PAID BY EAGLES WHO GAVE THEIR LIFE AND FELL
DEAD YET, PROUD THAT THEY FOUGHT SO WELL
GOLD, SILVER, NOR DIAMONDS WILL DO
THE PRICE HAS TO BE PAID BY ME AND YOU

BLACKMAN, WHITEMAN, JEWS, AND GENTLES
WE ALL MUST MAKE THIS PAYMENT WITH A SMILE
THAT PRICELESS GEM WE'LL HAVE TO PAY
WITH OUR LIVES TODAY AND EVERYDAY

NOW YOU KNOW WHAT MUST BE DONE
BY ME, YOU AND EVERYONE
IF WE WANT TO LIVE FREE, WE MUST FEARLESSLY SACRIFICE
CAUSE *"FREEDOM HAS A PRICE"*

A SOLDIER'S PRAYER

Mother please say a prayer for me
Cause I'm off to war far overseas
My M 1 rifle I'll carry in my hand
If I have to die, I'll die like a man

As bombs and bullets are aimed at me
If I die maybe I'll really be free
But I'm here to defend my home land
That's why this M1 rifle's in my hand

Me and my brothers know where we came from
And we know what we have to do
Hurry home to see mom
And defend other people like you

Don't worry Mom I 'll make it home
As long as God all mighty is on his throne
You see that bullet knows no color
If it strikes me, I'll die like my white brother

Oh mother, oh mother I call out your name
But way over here it's just not the same
While I kneel on my knees and pray
I pray that God will see me through the next war torn day

MIGHTY MO'S

Everybody open up your eyes and ears
I got something I want you to see and hear
It's about a place
That's far from disgrace

Where you can sit on your big or little ass
And smoke all the latest grass
Cosmic creatures crawling on the walls
Some seeming ten feet tall
Frankenstein is dancing the shimmy
And Dracula hollowing to you "give me"

Down at Mighty Mo's
Where everything go's
People don't care what you do
Some are going to make love to you
Hair hanging from here to there
People from everywhere

Young ladies they'll all be there
Some of all sizes and so fair
There's all you can drink
Drink so much till you can't think
Don't be surprised at who you might see
There's President Biden saying "excuse me"

Down at Mighty Mo's
Where everything go's
People don't care what you do
Some are going to make love to you
Hair of all colors hanging from here to there
People from everywhere

Take a look around
Your ears bulge from rhythmic sounds
You Take a look off to your right
You are Amazed, The Viet Cong soul band is out of sight

TAKE A WALK THROUGH YOUR HEART AND SEE IF THERE IS A PART THAT STILL LOVES ME

You left me all alone here crying
To call you back would be no use trying
As I sit here writing this letter
I hope you feel much, much better
If you would, just do this one last thing for me

Take a walk through your heart
And see if there is a part
That still loves me

It will not take long
I know I did you wrong
While you were away
And to this moment I regret it each day
But wait! Here's my soul for you to take
Do what you please with it
I don't care anymore, since I can't live with it
But please! Just do this one last thing for me
Take a walk through your heart
And see if there's a part

That still loves Jimmy

I'M GOING TO LIFT YOU UP FOR THE WHOLE WORLD TO SEE

I love you, I love you
Baby you are the whole world to me
With every little thing that you do
Girl, it's true I'll always love you

I'm going to lift you up
For the whole Universe to see
What a great beautiful thing that
Has happened to me

The world had labeled me a playboy
Every woman played with my heart like a used toy
Even though it was told to you
You still love me through and through

I'm going to lift you up
For the whole world to see
What a beautiful thing that
Has happened to me

From the top of mt Everest I will yell
My love story of you I will tell
I love you, I love you

I'M YOUR PASSPORT TO PLEASURE LAND

If you feel that this world is getting you down
Everything is foggy for miles around
Come and follow me
I have a place for you to see

I'm your passport to Pleasure Land
I'll do anything that you command
We'll do so many great things for pleasure
This land you will always treasure
All of the frustrations of this life will be put at ease
Cause you can be assured I have everything to please

Get yourself up and start to run
Don't worry baby there's plenty of fun
Widows, single girls, mothers to be
Come, come and follow me
I'm not choicy about this place
Come every sweet young thing from every race

I'm your passport to pleasure land
I'll do anything that you command
We'll do so many great things of pleasure
This land you will always treasure
All of the frustrations of this life will be put at ease
Cause you can be assured I have everything to please

SCORPIO

Ladies, There's only one thing you can do about him
Put on your track shoes women and run away
Cause if you're afraid of pure love
This man is the one you should leave alone any day

Passion means love and rules his incredible game
Satisfying ladies is this man's middle name
Do not stair into his hypnotics' eyes
You'll suddenly find yourself mesmerized
Scorpio is the deadliest male alive

To him everything is real not just jive
He's not afraid to express himself
He'll pull your glamourous love right off its lofty shelf

If he makes up his mind lady that he must have you
You can wager your heart lady the prophecy will come true
He'll embrace you just like an exclusive delicate flower
Love you more and more with each passing hour

Fall in love that he will never do
Make passionate sweet young love is all he wants to do
Chasing every sweet young lady around Tampa town
And make passionate love to each for miles around

Scorpio is the deadliest male alive
To him everything is real and not just jive
He's not afraid to express himself
He'll pull your exclusive love ladies, right off its lofty shelf

THE SHADOW

The massive Shadow came out of nowhere
It rose up and suddenly swept me away
We traveled a very, very long time
It must have been for several days

Then the Shadow came to an abrupt thunderous stop
High, high upon the tallest mountain top
The shadow then sternly pointed at the world below
And slowly sank his massive lengthy index finger low and low

The Shadow pointed down into a world size deep dark horrible pit'
Towards an ungodly horrible place I don't ever want to go
As Tears began filling my eyes
I started to unmercifully cry
I asked the Shadow, please tell me the reasons why

The immense Shadow sternly looked down at tiny me and began in his thunderous voice
A voice so Loud the whole universe could hear since it roared from each and
Every mountain top and corner of the universe without a choice
It thundered, Prostitution, revolution, segregation, discrimination, war, hunger, genocide
Murder, greed, corruption, Bonded to their soul,
Adulteresses are so bold,
Liars proudly speak openly , and have no respect for me
Man going places where he doesn't belong
It's okay if it's in search my throne

Blast Fleming, stealing, and going with each other's wives
No one has no room for the great book they think it just jives
Passion to one's color
Don't dare call me brother
No respect for older folk
Everything they say is just a joke

Science claim's you started from an artificial cell
When it is I who put you together so well
I created you in the images of me
But you've gone too far left you see
The Shadow then took me back to the place where it got me from
I frantically reached out and touched it's enormous arm
I said please shadow does the world have a chance to rearrange
Is there time for the world to change

The mountainous Shadow slowly looked conscientiously down at tiny me
And voice thundered the world has time to be saved from a fiery grave,
But mankind better hurry, cause I'm starting to get mentally worried

LOVE ADVICE

Hey man, stop assaulting on that woman.
Assaulting her and acting like a caveman.
You're only messing up your love.
Man that isn't no way to treat one of God's doves
If she did you wrong, assaulting her isn't going to change the situation
Correct her and improve your infatuation
You see I'm telling you this for This reason.

I once loved this woman.
One does not know what love is until it's
wrecked your home, tear apart your heart
leaves you for dead, And not a single tear shed

JAMES M. MOTEN 73

Cause love is a very personal fling,
Something that makes one do lots of crazy things
love can make you rich, love can make you poor.
Love can be the thin dividing line between love and hate
Be the provider of Success, the teller of one's fate.
I once was a whole man, able to lift up my head, and feel sorrow
laugh At the sound of joy
Look at me now, I've lost my will to live

I once loved this woman
You don't know what hurt is until it's
wrecked your home, tore apart your heart, left you for dead
And not a single tear shed

Even though I was man enough to walk away
I made the mistake and turned and looked Back
Many times I tried again and again to rack this woman
Remove my cloak of caveman
Listen Mister be more of a man than I am
That's it, walk away and don't look Back. Not today or any day.

Now your home won't be wrecked, your heart is still in one part
You will not be left for dead
Now a tear she will shed

KEEP ON IT

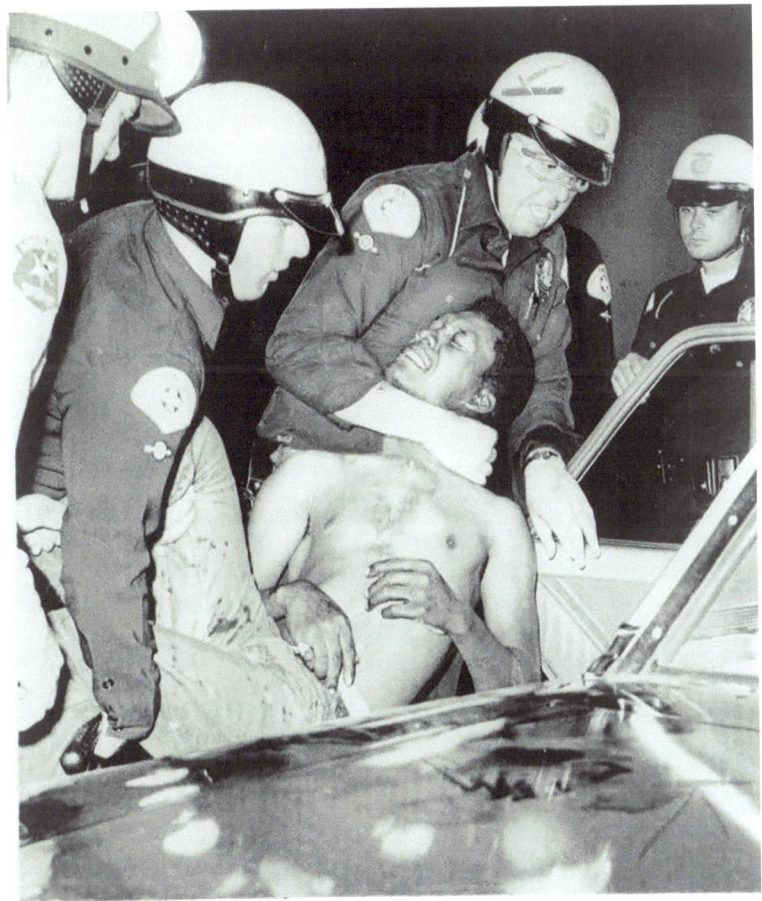

We hear a lot of people yelling
About all their good and bad times
Opening up their mouths super wide
Trying to get on your good side

You cannot be overly concerned black people
Trying to get to your personal groove
In reality you might be too high my brother
To make the right move

Keep on it, I know it is violent at times my brother
Trying to get it all out
But you must Keep on it
I know it is trying my sister
Trying to progress and only getting so far
We all have time my people
To get the funk out

When you finally wake up and take time to realize
You then pump yourself up and with a scholastic smile
Cystically conclude, and abundantly realize
You've always had victory over the man and his aggressive styles

FOOLED AGAIN

Sitting here in this gloomy room
Sipping on a tall glass of J & B
Feeling full of gloom
Things just didn't work out for me
Maybe the answer is in this I'm drinking
One thing for sure I'm thinking
About me and you
And how it could have been
If you had only been true

I have dedicated my whole life to you
To cherish and worship everything that you do
But there came along another
With words of sugar and a four leaf clover
You quickly made your choice
Either me or his Rolls Royce

The pain I can never tell
It's something that will never get well
As I look up in the sky towards heaven
This time my dice didn't roll seven nor eleven
You waved good bye to me as you road down the road
This ends the fooled again saddest love story ever told

THE HARD LIFE WOMAN

Please don't look down at me that way
I'm a better woman than you have ever seen any day
I was forced out into these Chicago streets
I make my living on my back then change these sheets
My life has been hard from the beginning
Before I was fourteen I was earning a living

JAMES M. MOTEN   79

My mother died from drugs when that child was born
My father he was already old and worn
I have seven brothers and sisters who needed to be fed
That is why I'm in this hell ridden bed

With no one to turn to
Oh lord what could I do
I found myself out there on the ghettos blocks
That's why I'm lying here with someone like you

My block business has done all right
Ten and two, have been out of sight
Go ahead mister and look down on me
I got no other choice you see

I swore I'd never let a day go by
That the sound of hunger they would cry
I know a blessing's going to come my way
And God be my helper I 'll leave this hell ridden bed that day

DON'T DOWN YOUR BROTHER CAUSE HE IS TRYING TO MOVE FURTHER

DEAL WITH PEOPLE
WHO PUTS YOU DOWN

There's a sister who is a movie star
There's a brother who just hit a baseball so far
There go's George Hood
Driving his new Cadillac Fleetwood
There's Willie, Joe, and Pete squawking
Sister Sara, Mrs. Johnson and company are talking

They can be no future friends of mine
I knew they had money all the time
Licking those uppity white folks ass
I knew all the time, they weren't just over there mowing their grass

I know how she got that new furniture
Old uppity nigger's secret ten and two
I'm glad that isn't what me and you do

Ma' ma, Ma' ma, come and see
Mrs. Wilson's getting a new T.V.
You children just stay at home
For over there no more you will Rome

Billy and Darlene are in their third year of college
Their mother's making them get that knowledge
I guess soon they'll be acting like they are so much
The inside of her house I'll no longer touch
I'm going to tell the welfare woman they got a new TV.
I knew all the time, her doing house work wasn't cheap you see

This mourning Victoria was chosen Queen at her school
This afternoon she looked toward us as if we are fools

Jody's mama better put a mattress on her back
She's already made enough to get all they lack
Oh honey, I'm glad you know what's going on
Honey, You need to be sitting next to God on his throne

I'm filled with the holy ghost and fire
This body of mind will never be for hire

Sister Tapley's husband show is fine
If I was not saved child, he'd sure be mine
Sister you don't mean that, we both are too fat
Don't worry baby fat is where it's at

do not down your brother cause he tries to move further
No matter how he or she did it
They found the way to make it fit

PLEASE DON'T COME TOMORROW
(TRY AND STAY TODAY)

shutterstock.com · 695813362

Come tomorrow that lady, she will leave me
She says she's tired of my love and wants to be free
She said maybe we will find each other someday
Lord knows I must find a way to get her to stay

Please do not come tomorrow
Please do not come tomorrow
Try and stay today
Oh lord how I wish she wouldn't leave me this way

She is the only woman I have ever loved
Worshipped and adored like heaven above
But my love she needs no longer
Weak, but I will get stronger

Please do not come tomorrow
Please do not come tomorrow
Try and stay today
Oh lord, how I wish she wouldn't leave me this way

I know I cannot stop God's clock
Each minute that clock ticks off
Is a minute my heart stops
I have little time to try and rearrange
To pray and get us to change

Please do not come tomorrow
Try and stay today
Please do not come tomorrow
I must keep her someway
Please do not come tomorrow
Please change your mind girl
Please do not come tomorrow
Try and stay today

IS IT THE WRONG LIFE?

It's a long hard road to the top
I'm going to keep on pushing and not stop
I came a long way to get where I am today
I loss blood, flesh, and tears along the way

JAMES M. MOTEN   85

I wish I could find a place
A place for a lost race
Sometimes I hate I was born black
So many things I seem to lack

All the time there's an unjust dark cloud imposed around me
Symbolizing I will never be free
Every way I seem to turn
People disliking me will they ever learn

Change colors that I would never do
Change so I can pursue happiness the same as you
I've been hurt so many times, it no longer matter
If given happiness, I would not accept it, even on a gold platter

People think I'm the outcast
Something that does not belong, from the prehistoric past
I've suffered to long and too hard in this land
No one to turn to, to mend my wounds, nor lend me a helping hand

Sometimes I wished to the almighty God up above that my mother had made a short
Grave the day I was born
Raised in this world to face hardships
I cannot express the feelings which lay upon my lips

Branded and labeled before I was born
My life was already set and torn
Left for dead and little desire
Extra, extra, here's a modern day slave for hire

Discriminated against continuously
My clothes are too fancy for me to be black
Things like that I'm supposed to lack
If I could be you and you could be me
For just one day of my ghetto life then you'll see

GOT TO FIND MY SELF A STEADY LOVE

Up and down these same old funky Tampa, Florida streets
These same old funky Broadway streets
Drinking and raising hell
I'm getting so tired, I think I'll just yell

Got to find myself a steady love
All this running around is blowing my mind
I've Wasted all my money, killed all my time
I've got to find myself a steady love

I've made sweet love to every Florida woman I see
Lord have mercy it's starting to get next to me
There was a time when I could stay out all night
Dancing, raising hell and getting into fights

I've got to find myself a steady love
Help. Help, young ladies come running fast
All you pretty sweet young ladies I know will last
Twenty-four hours of love you'll be guaranteed
Then a little overtime yes indeed

Lord knows I got to find myself a steady love
Won't some lady help me please
Show me someone to put my mind at ease

My money has gotten low, and low
The Davis Island Doctors say you have no more blood to sell
The credit union says your account is dry as an Arizona desert well
Your Commander has ordered you to let the Sarasota, Florida women go

I've got to find myself a steady love
I've got to find myself a steady love

THE WELFARE WOMAN

Welfare Reform

Important Events

Welfare reform

What:
The Personal Responsibility and Work Opportunity Reconciliation Act of 1996 reforms welfare

Who:
Passed by Congress and signed into law by President Bill Clinton

When:
Signed on August 22, 1996

Before 1750
1750-1799
1800-1849
1850-1899
1900-1924
1925-1949
1950-1974
1975-2000

A New Beginning
Welfare to Work

Tucson Welfare women get away from my La Reforma door
Do not come around here anymore
But I guess if it is not for you
I would not have anything to eat
I'm too young to care or do
Or whether I'm clean or neat

Each time you come I have to hide the used Television
I wish you did not mind
Mom says you might take away our check
Then she says we will surely be in a wreck

With eight months to feed
One-hundred and sixty-one dollars we need
So I guess I have to be content
To sit and smell this stinky rat scent

Roaches and huge bugs throughout the house
With little room for me, let alone several mouse
President Eisenhower if you can hear my plea
Tell the welfare woman to join your army

One day I'll become a man
Then I'll earn a living with my own two hands

CAUSE I BELIEVE

I know that there is a place for me
A place where I can really be free
I know I must get to Graceland someway
If not tomorrow, then the very next day

IT'S OKAY TO OPEN YOUR EYES IN THIS CASE LADY JUSTICE

Cause I believe out beyond the vast America horizon
That there is a place beyond comparison
A place where we will talk women to man
And neither claims to have an upper hand

I believe it is a magnificent place for me and a wonderful place for you
A place for the white woman, black woman and the Jew
It takes a beautiful dream to get us there
It's a place where everyone really cares

Cause I believe out beyond the vast American horizon
That there is a marvelous place beyond comparison
A place where we can simply talk women to man
And neither claims to have an upper hand

As we close our eyes and begin our dream
We will be there in a moment as it seems
When we awaken women to man you'll see
That you, and you only loves me

LOVE THE CHILDREN

Gods Precious little ones
With eyes of brown. Black, hazel and blue
You can be sure
That God loves you

Love the children
Love the children

Gods precious little ones
The future is truly theirs
When it's all said and done

Love the children
Love the children

Not a care in their little hearts
Not having a single worry on their young mind
Out in the bright sunshine, they will run and play
Laughing and singing the day away

Love the children
Love the children

God's precious little ones
The future is theirs
When it's all said and done

Love the children
Love the children

Remember you were a child once
Laughing playing under the sun
Your precious mother set your destiny
And loved you each and everyone

Love the children
Love the children

OLD MAN TIME

Have you ever been in love
Wake up one morning and find
That the one you love is not really on your mind
As You lie awake, and think about the times

Your mind journey's back to younger days
When you begged God to let you make it
You really did not care about the time
Nor the place,
Just loving the one next to you with god given grace

Time is like a wonderer
pausing here and then there, but not really going nowhere
You would catch a boat, hitch a ride
Spend your last dollar and salvage my pride
Just to get home to her

Go back old man to your younger days
Cause you can now look back and proudly say
Thank you God I made it

One day lady luck spent some time with me
And I made it to the tallest mountain top
Now, as I set with old man time at my side
I return to loving just you

Go back old man to younger days
Cause you and I, can look around and proudly say
Oh lord thank you so very much, I've made it

Author: JAMES MARVIN MOTEN

ALSO DEDICATED TO THE GOD GIVEN FOLLOWING

JAMES M. MOTEN'S

HISTORY OF FAMILY SERVICE IN THE UNITED STATES

ARMED FORCES

1. CLYDE HARRIS, UNCLE, HONORABLE, USA, WWII, ALL BLACK 4TH ARMY INVASION OF ITALY. Buried military section Evergreen Cemetery Tucson.

2. MOSE HARRIS, UNCLE, HONORABLE, USN, WWII, served in Pacific, served on Midway Aircraft Carrier. Buried military section of San Diego Cemetery.

3. ROSE HARRIS, AUNT, wife of MOSE HARRIS, she was a riveter during WWII at Solar Aircraft Corporation San Diego, Ca. Fighter planes, bombers. She is buried next to my UNCLE.

4. BOOKER HARRIS, UNCLE, HONORABLE, USMC, WWII, served in Pacific buried military section Los Angeles Cemetery.

5. BOBBIE R. MOTEN, BROTHER, HONORABLE, USAF, Korea War, Vietnam War, Buried military section Evergreen Cemetery Tucson. Crewman C-141. Died 1973 over China Sea of heart attack during his 4th trip in 10 days flying POW's home. I am investigating the Gold Star Standards since I misplaced copies of paperwork given to my mother at the time.

6. JAMES M. MOTEN, 3 HONORABLE, USAF, USMC (ICELAND), USA, Vietnam Era, Cold War. Recognized by Certificate Chuck Hagel. Secretary of Defense United States, and the Secretary of Treasury, Retired IRS Agent, Michael Dillon Award winner, Benjamin Gallatin Award winner, In excess of 150 IRS awards.

7. ELLIOT M. MOTEN, SON, HONORABLE, USA, FT HOOD, TEXAS 2 TOURS IRAQ, 1TOUR AFGHANISTAN, Kosovo, and BLACKHAWK CREW CHIEF (585 Combat Flight Hours earning the Sikorsky Flight Medal, 20+ Retired Master Sergeant, received Congratulation letter from President Donald Trump.
Picture of ELLIOT M. MOTEN next page, big pilot next to helicopter.

8. SHAWN M. MOTEN, SON, HONORABLE, USN, USA, 3 TOURS IRAQ.

9. JOHN W. MOTEN, SON, HONORABLE, USMC, Injured 8th week boot camp, Honorable Discharge. Disabled Veteran.

10. WARFELD M. MOTEN, SON, HONORABLE, USMC, USA 1 Tour, IRAQ wounded.

11. STEPHANIE TATORA GRANDDAUGHTER, HONORABLE, USA, Ft Carson, Colorado active duty. Now serving in the USAF.

12. NICOLAS STACHELEK GRANDSON, HONORABLE, USA, 38th Parallel, Korea active duty.
13. MICAH MOTEN, NEPHEW, HONORABLE, USA, 4 Tours Iraq.
In loving memory of my precious nephew who served the United States faithfully. I copied The following from my precious sister Dr. Darlene Moten his mother's obituary September 2023.
'God allowed me to know you almost 33 years!!! He allowed you to serve two tours in Afghanistan. You flew on helicopters, worked near land mines, and saw others wounded and killed. God spared your life.
Resting in peace Evergreen Cemetery Tucson, Arizona
14. ZEQUISTA ANNMARIE HOOPER, GRANDDAUGHTER, HONORABLE, USMC, Camp Pendleton, Ca. Afghanistan, currently in Korea. Transferred to ARMY.
15. EDDIE HARRIS TATE, USMC, COUSIN, HONORABLE, Oakland, Ca. 2 tours Vietnam War disabled.
16. ELMER HARRIS, COUSIN, HONORABLE, USA, 2 Tours Vietnam, Buried Military section Houston Cemetery.

God be with them all.

Author: JAMES MARVIN MOTEN

MSGT ELLIOTT M MOTEN

MICAH MOTEN

loving In loving memory of my precious nephew who served the United States faithfully. I copied The following from my precious sister Dr. Darlene Moten his mother's obituary September 2023. 'God allowed me to know you almost 33 years!!! He allowed you to serve two tours in Afghanistan. You flew on helicopters, worked near land mines, and saw others wounded and killed. God spared your life.

Your Uncle James M Moten